Mickey Brown

My life through poetry

To my great friend, the legend Mick Kirby
Thank You for everything.

Published by Mickey Brown

Publishing partner: Paragon Publishing, Rothersthorpe
First published 2021

© Mickey Brown 2021

ISBN 978-1-78222-884-4

Book design, layout and production management by Into Print
www.intoprint.net
+44 (0)1604 832149

Contents

About Me 5

WORLD EVENTS

Spring in the Air 9

Thank You Our NHS 11

Ready Brex 12

Peace of Mind 14

Honour 16

WTF ! 17

It's Just Not Cricket 18

Maggie, May I ? 20

Act One Act Now 21

Return Our Dogs 23

Hurry Up England, Now is the Time 24

Theresa May 25

FAMILY

Mum's the Word 29

Miss King 30

Robin Reliant 31

Festive Feelings 32

Don't Worry Be Happy 33

Auntie Patsy So Bright 34

Isaac Michael Eric 35

Autumn Feelings 36

These Diamonds are Forever 38

Kidford 40

January 42

CANCER

You are my World 45

We will C 46

Driving 47

What a Day 48

CONTENTS

Richard the Lionheart. 49

'C' Bomb. .. .. .50

Moment of Sadness. 52

Wally 53

Well Done Dad 54

Thames Hospice. 55

SADNESS

'Small' Spring is in the Air 59

My Mate Scrubble. 60

Breakfast at Tiffany's 62

Pixie 64

P.C. 66

CELEBRITIES

Mega Dump 69

Pardon ? Eh, what did you say ? 70

Team Ditcheat. 72

The Gypsy King. 74

Caroline Flack.. 76

Voice is the Choice 77

MENTAL HEALTH

Losing It.. 81

Always Got A Chance. 82

One Life, Live It. 84

HUMOUR

Weight Watchers. 87

Superhali Fragilistic Smells Like Halitosis 88

Justice 89

Hair Hair. 90

Team Rosebank 92

To My Editor, The Lovely Coleen 93

About Me

After watching my Mum at the typewriter as a child I was unaware that she was writing poetry. Sometime later I sat down and read the results of her efforts. This gave me the inspiration and motivation to write my own.

Over the years I realise it was poetry that has helped me through life's ups and downs; being a comfort during difficult times but also fun and uplifting in happier times.

My experiences in life are outlined in this book, from family to world events and sadly cancer which has featured too.

I live in Berkshire with my partner, our Chihuahua called Tiffany Brown, and Colin, our cat. I have a young son, Isaac.

I specialise in writing poetry – both personal and for businesses. I also write jingles, strap and tag lines for clients.

I've had previous work published in books and newspapers and featured on radio and TV.

I hope that you enjoy reading my book and thank you for taking the time to do so.

Mickey

Mickey with his Mum, Patsy

WORLD EVENTS

Spring in the Air

(The Pandemic)

I woke at 5 a.m. this morning
To the birds singing in the trees
I laid back in my sack with my ears pinned back
Like a concert with no entry fees

The silence was golden
With that lick of clean spring air
Just the song from a Thrush and her mates, it was lush
They were Two Metres apart to be fair

The morning dew on the grass
Then the blue sky just appeared
Not a cloud in sight now the bird's songs slight
Like a support act for the gig we had cheered

For a moment in these sad times
I was free from all the hype
The negative news and the smouldering fuse
That seems to be smoked in a not-so-peace pipe

I thought long about my family
My lovely mother, dearest friends, some foe
My gorgeous son and his incredible mum
Let this virus turn around and go !

My work colleagues, my lovely neighbours
Did they hear the same as me?
With the early song birds not short on words
Chirping from the top of the trees

For what is going on out there?
This morning's gig instilled great vibes
We are safe at home like a dog with a bone
For our NHS we are full of pride

Hats off to all our Posties
On the front line been selected
From our young and old some all alone
They've help keep us all connected

Hats off to these volunteers
Like worker bees to their queen's new hive
They now take to the zone not a hint of a drone
To help keep our human race alive

What heart and pride they show
Please all return fit and well
We can all reflect and show pure respect
Let's pray there's no sequel!

2020

THANK YOU
OUR NHS

Hats off to our NHS
Our Paramedics and Frontline Nurses
Our Doctors and our Surgeons
Who have been facing viral curses
You go out to work daily
As one united medical team
You all play your parts with your purple hearts
So selfless in your means

Please also spare a thought
For the hospital Porters and Cleaners too
As they oil the wheels in their trusted fields
To beat this Corona virus Flu
Thank the Hospital shop attendants
Serving goods and papers to the sick
The security guards who play their cards
To watch over with a moral tick

The staff in the hospital restaurants
Who feed and nourish their medical teams
Providing a service second to none
Willing a C19 virus ending dream
From admission through to discharge
And every employee in between
We thank you our NHS with your Lion hearts
That makes you our Winning Team !

2021

Ready Brex

I woke up this morning
Was it Breakfast or a Brexit?
Like so many and if I'm right
We've made the perfect Exit !

Scaremongering politicians
Propaganda is their feed
When it's all about the money
And eternal greed

Our pound will end up stronger
Ok it's hitched a blip
But just look at the Euro now
It's about to have a kip !

We can now guard our borders
And tick that off our list
So from now on who enters here
Will face the tightened fist !

We are so proud of England
At last we've found our voice
The voice of our people
They've made the perfect choice

An Englishman's home is his Castle
So the saying goes
Our families our children and theirs too
To be safe not on their toes !

Living under threat
Of who is coming here next
We've now half a chance to make a stance
And be so much more select !

We created the National Health
Now with it we're bemused
As it's become International Health
And been totally abused !

We live in a Democracy
With a Text it or a Tweet
We're entitled to our freedom of speech
Let's stand on our own two feet !

We're split with our decisions
But as a Nation we are one
Once the dust settles, and it will
You will see that we have Won !

25/06/2016

Peace of mind

RIP Lee Rigby

Well what a World we live in
Brought up to be kind and giving
When on the streets in any town
There should be no fear for the living

A soldier joins the forces
Because he has belief
To protect and serve his country
With that element of grief

Afghanistan, the Taliban
Either of – we're not a fan
We sometimes ask ourselves, what's it all about
An eye for an eye disgusts me, easier ways to sort it out

Our serving soldier lays dead
Off duty after his shift
Defenceless having time out
To be set upon by extremists

Think before you act
There is a battlefield
Where there's a fifty-fifty chance
To face your foe with shield

Don't bring it to our streets
For our younger generation
To witness mindless violence
And disrupt their happy nation

I see pictures in the paper
Of murdered lad Lee Rigby
What did he do to you personally
It's callous, cold so sickly

You've had your fix for now
We're sick to the pit and sad
Cos you've left his wife a widow
And a son without a dad !

(24/05/13)

Honour

*In Honour of our WW1 Hero Ancestors and their
War Horses*

One Hundred years on
One Hundred years ago
We owe our lives to those that fought and fell
In battle toe to toe

Our equine friends amongst them
Trudging through the mud
Risking life and limb chance of survival slim
Shedding sweat and tears and blood

We take so much for granted
Though back then a different story
Yet in a way come ration day
In itself worth the fight for Glory

We thank you for our freedom
Where would we be without you
At just the thought our hearts they sink
For the sacrifices that you went through

We are proudly here today
To celebrate their lives
They walked and fought, we in honour talk
About those brave men and their wives.

WTF !
2020

What a sad old World we live in
We're just taking now, not giving
Brexit first that quenched our thirst
Corona now affects the lives we're living!

To hear football's been cancelled
The rugby's followed suit
No Grand National, no Tiger Roll
Euros 2020 now on mute!

No pubs for a social bevvy
No restaurants for a date
No Theatre 🎭 dreams nor Silver Screens!
Our Country's in a right old state!

The world is under pressure
To clean up this viral act
We need to get to grips and wipe our lips.
Break it's back and that's a fact!

Our home is where the heart is
Be kind and show affection
We need to do what's right to end this fight!
Help bring back true perfection!

It's Just Not Cricket

(Theresa May PM 21/11/2018)

When you are so close to achieving something
Then part of your team fail in support
You need extra cover from the silly mid off
Then phrase a suitably cutting retort !

You have to wear your batting pads
Then the faceguard as a shield
A deep square you are not Mrs May
You're like the umpire in this field

As you stroll on into bat
And take aim from the crease
They will not bowl this maiden over
Whilst you're trying to restore calm and peace !

The bowler leg spins one towards you
You hit a six into the thicket
The opposition have crossed the boundary
Now they are on a sticky wicket !

The sight screen's there for a reason
Backstabbers hide behind and bicker
Yet you are on the pitch in play
Cheered on by Lords and the local vicar

Theresa it's you that's showing resolve
And amazing strength in depth
Some dip their toe then run a mile
Yet you've gone the length and breadth

The new team you have beside you
Will hopefully bring a bit of clout
You've done your best in this final test
Please don't Boycott as you're Not Out !

Maggie, May I ?

PLEASE wake up Maggie, I think I've got questions to put to you
It's the beginning of June and right now, I'm feeling a bit of a fool
I clearly lit the fuse, but now I'm completely bemused
Oh Maggie, I think I could have tried - a little more …

I don't want to bleat or have a good moan,
I just want to keep number '10' as my home !
Some felt I played a bit part and that's what really hurts !

The morning sun shining on my face –
With too many late nights, really shows my age
But deep in my heart I am so full of rage

With Labour firmly stuck in my throat
And with 'Her' constant moaning, from John O'Groats
Oh Maggie I could have tried, a little more.

I refuse to give up my home,
To a smiling and smug garden gnome
Who borrowed some of my poll
And that's a gain I can do without !

All I need now is a friend to help me make amends with a guiding hand
With Brexit so near I must instil calm with no fear and get my head out
the sand
We've all got a job to do and fulfil our Country's expectations in Blue !

Oh Maggie ' T ' I'm going to try a load more
I can't bear the thought of losing my home,
To a smiling and smug garden gnome

No 10's in my heart
I couldn't leave it if I tried !

10/06/17

Return Our Dogs

You are worse than scum
Just manure under your shoe
If you knew the heartfelt impact
Of stealing 'Dogs For You'

Dogs are like peoples' babies
A friend for life indeed
Especially through this lockdown
Not for your eternal greed

Think of something else
Don't steal from your own
You steal a pet from it's home
You have no morals atone

You break the hearts of many
With a target that is easy
A dog's for life not Christmas
A buck for you it's easy

Well please give a thought to your victims
It doesn't matter about their wealth
They may be simply hanging on to life
Due to mental health !

2021

Act One Act Now

My heartfelt condolences to all the families involved in Monday's atrocity in the Manchester Arena

Are we going round in circles
Are we simply stunned by fear
Atrocities somewhere once a month
Were all shedding lots of tears !
We are the greatest proudest nation
We congregate in mass
After Monday's dire event once more
What's going on is crass !

Someone needs to stand up
Let's temporary waiver human rights
As that has been the main excuse
Favouring the terrorists at night !
We've got Piers Morgan chomping
With the support from Ben and Kate
Colonel Richard Kemp now firing
To slam shut the terror gate !

This is such a huge step forward
As more people share their choice
The way it's going like the Monteverdi Choir
We can support and back their voice
Manchester we love you
As London we do too
From John O'Groats to Lands End
Let's no longer take a view !

These were our beloved children
All singing dancing having fun
Then some evil force with no remorse
Scowled like a mad dog with a gun !
What was his reason
I can't fathom it not fully
A disciple NO! a coward YES!
A vulgar fiend and bully !

We now need to deal the cards
And make sure they are in our favour
As what's gone on is vile so wrong
It's left a distasteful awful flavour
We now need a quick solution
Hunt and face them with our guns
They will fade and die no battle cry
Clean air once more - rid of pollution !

So moving forward swiftly
Let's now get our plans in place
And bring back miles of junior smiles
Put happiness back on their face !
We are such a tight knit nation
Who will only take so much
We will conquer them - undo their hem
Great Britain let's go Dutch !

22/05/2017

Hurry up England Now is the Time

We're a Nation in desperation
Shattered dreams lost reputation
All the hype it came to pass
To this day a total farce

Our loyal fans keep on believing
Their hard earned money now they're grieving
Recession times they feel the pain
No rainbow glowing just cloud and rain

What's it all about Alfie 'R'
You had class and no fast cars
The party's solemn, far from a rave
I hope you haven't turned in your grave

Sir Alf just sprinkle golden dust
Cos Wednesday's Win is now a must
No heart no fire in the belly
Its Rock and Roll to smash your telly

There's people risking daily life
2 years and more without a wife
Some come home some laid to rest
Give them a thought and play your best

Times are hard you are having fun
Just pass the ball and run and run
Don't waste this chance to stand and fight
Our Country's waning, put it right !!

18/06/2010

Theresa May

Well done you Theresa
You've had your back against the wall
You've proved some doubters oh so wrong
Now rise - stand firm and tall

Since you came to power
Earning your place at number ten
No easy ride you refuse to hide
You sharpened your pencil, dipped your pen.

It's been a mountain like no other
So testing like Everest
But shoulders back, taken on the chin
Your proving you're the best !

With so many having faith in you
My loyal family for one
There's times we've sat, watched some vile spats
Now it's them that turn and run !

You are proving daily
Given time to find your feet
You face things head on you're so on song
It's others hearts that skip a beat !

You've had some hurdles from the start
You had brick walls along the way
But from me to you in all you do
Congratulations Theresa May !

19/03/2018

FAMILY

Mum's The Word

Happy Mother's Day

You are such an incredible lady
There is no better word
You always listen to our voice
When it's you that should be heard
We always come to you
As you're a wealth of precision knowledge
You are always right with such insight
Your brain's like Eton College
We appreciate your love, your instinct as our Mum
I would give you anything from protection, laughter, fun
The strength that you show in any given situation
Is just pure class in a glass You'd feed a starving nation
Your company is special, culinary delights a must
But your mind is kindest of them all
In your love and words we trust
I just have to say on your special day
We're so proud of you, with a huge THANK YOU !
I adore you in every way.
Happy Mother's Day.

30/03/14

Miss King

(Isaac, my 6-year-old son's teacher)

Miss King you've been exceptional
Throughout these testing times
You've cared and shared for our children
In fact you've been sublime
Your teaching job is never easy
It takes such dedication
Especially throughout this pandemic phase
In itself an education
We personally want to thank you
For your commitment through the years
You will be missed, at the top of our list
I'm sure there will be a few tears

2021

Robin Reliant

I want to share this with you
And you need to know
How brill you are and how good you've been
To let your Robbie go !

There's no one that feels more gutted
Than you Patsy, Caz and me
You brought him back from the reaper's grasp
To dancing on your knee !

What you achieved for him
A bird on his last legs
Is truly so amazing
With mealworms and a comfy bed !

Don't be sad my lovely
Cos you are the best
Whatever's thrown you never moan
You've always passed the sternest tests !

All I want to say is
Thank you for all you are
If I achieve an ounce of yours
Then I will go so far !

So rest up now my lovely
You can hit the sack
Knowing he's only in your garden
And he will soon be back !

Festive Feelings

The Christmas strain's approaching
When your purse strings do need coaching
Too easy to groan take out a loan
As the lenders are just poaching.

Think of all the good things
Family, friends and love
They cost very little if nothing
Don't fall for the verse above

It's a time for fun and games
Please don't feel the stress
Keep your loved ones nice and close
Don't end up in a mess !

Merry Christmas

(11/12/13)

Don't Worry Be Happy

(To my Dad…having a moan)

Life is short life is sweet
With it's ups and downs
You once told me we're from good stock
From the loins of Johnny Brown

We cling to that thought
Whatever's thrown we'll catch it
So if you're feeling like a moan
Pick up the phone we'll match it !!

You are no spring chicken
Take each day as it comes
To wake up is a bonus
With teeth still in your gums

You are still a leader
And that you'll always be
With positive thoughts, your mental strength
You're still the same J.B.

So think before you speak
As you drilled that into me
Look forward not backwards
Drop the moaning H.J.C.

'Keep your pecker up !!'

Auntie Patsy So Bright

(To my lovely Auntie, Patsy Bright – aka Old Auntie Pat)

Good morning O.A.P
You mean the world to me
I love our chats so poss no spats
On all things we agree

I love your wit and charm
Never do anyone no harm
But in my book you've got the look
And that elegance and calm

Through our chats I learn a lot
Because you genuinely give a jot
You don't suffer fools drunk on bar stools
Or a know-all on a tot !

Life is a learning curve
And some have got a nerve
You do warn me of when to flee
And people I should swerve

I appreciate your drive
It's what keeps me alive
I've been through the mill without a pill
You give me strength to strive

So thank you for your kindness
Just you never change
From me to you I do love you
You are top of the range

Isaac Michael Eric

2017

Happy Christmas Isaac Bear
You really are so cute
You smile a mile show love with style
You really are a beaut !

Even though you can be naughty
Your spirit is a gift
That's what makes you who you are
You give everyone a lift !

You are nearly three
I am so proud of you son
The work and hours put into you
By your loving, caring Mum

You are such a clever boy
You can count, sing nursery rhymes
Ride your scooter in the park
We have such amazing times

I love you first thing in the morning
I love you all day and through the night
Happy Christmas Gorgeous Boy
Isaac you are my shining light !

All my love Daddy Bear xx

Autumn Feelings

For Isaac, my 5 year old son

It's Isaac's year 1 homework 📚
Autumn was his topic chosen
Quite a task from behind Miss King's mask 😷
As they all just stood there frozen 🥶

In Autumn leaves 🍂 are falling
Trees are left so bare
The birds take flight to a sunnier site
They are all so much happier there !

The hedgehogs 🦔 search for food
To store it with their mates
With winter here they have no fear
Cos they are off to hibernate !

The rabbits munch on grass
They find the freshest shoots
They hop and play then run away
Once they've filled their boots

The squirrels 🐿 gather their nuts
To save them for hibernation
They climb their trees, avoid the bees 🐝
To sleep with dedication !

The conkers are now falling
The sun is going down
The cold's arrived into our lives
As we stand there with a frown !

All is not lost

The dark nights are on our side
Halloween's here 🎃 projecting fear
The trick or treaters have arrived !

All of the above
Is such a learning tool
Your homework's complete  and what a feat
A fitting tribute to your school

Daddy

These Diamonds are Forever

Well what a brilliant lady
And what a brilliant gent
With Rob and Col it's meant to be
They are clearly so content !
Congratulations are in order
For this happy couple who are true
Like Eden Hazard and Diego Costa
Both loving Chelsea like they do !

Coleen makes people feel so special
She has this amazing gift
Down to the finer detail
That gives everyone a lift
What she's got in Robbie
Is one loyal loving man
They fit each other like a glove
To that I am a fan !

So you lovely couple
Lady Penelope and Parker
We wish you luck from in our hearts
Now from a Burbridge to a Barker
Congratulations Col and Robbie
On behalf of all us here
Enjoy your day and future too
You deserve the loudest cheer !

With Robbie's Art and Coleen's Flair
They are so humble yet so clever
Thank you both for being you !
These Diamonds are forever !
Now all I want to say is
It's your day now have some fun
And Robbie on your wedding night
Get in there my son !

22/04/2017

Kidford

On my sister, Caroline's birthday

Well where do I start
I guess at the beginning
When you popped out my little sis
We all just stood there brimming !

We have a little sister
Proud as punch we are
And as you grew we just knew
You are our little star !

I stand here so proud
As you soon found your feet
In difficult times you just marched on
Yet were always so discreet !

You are so amazing
Full of laughter and fun
But most of all hand on my heart
You are such a brilliant Daughter, Sister, Mum !

I am so proud to have you
But more so share our bond
And wouldn't change a thing
You are above and beyond !

So Happy Birthday Kidford
On your Special Day
We love you to bits with all your wits
Let's raise our glass, Hooray !

Happy Birthday to you my lovely little sis !

Thank you for everything…

January

With January now upon us
And another Christmas gone
The New Year chimes of better times
Our Mums and Dads deserve a gong !

All the excitement from our children
With Santa and his Elves
Wrapping final presents on Christmas Eve
Then sneak off to bed at Twelve !

We worked all year in the build up
Saving when and where we were able
To bring miles and miles of festive smiles
And put that turkey on the table !

As we start the New Year
It's cold and damp and wet
So wrap up warm in your hats, gloves and scarves
Now it's on your marks - get set !

The January Blues are approaching
Well as the saying goes
Much love to all happy times stay safe
Mums, Dads, Sisters and our Bros !

CANCER

You are my World

To think what you have been through
Not on your own but we too
That's you and me and Tiffany
One final push to pull through

Amazing strength you show
A heart of gold you flow
Today I'm sad and feeling bad
You're the world to us you know

My tears are of frustration
When results should show elation
Cos in my book you've got the look
Of a stunning dance formation !

If my heart strings went untouched
Be like 'thank you very much'
Heart on my sleeve not prepared to grieve
There's a final twist as such

The support you have's immense
Like a rope it's become tense
W'ere there for you, you always knew
We'd jump the highest fence

The words that they have spoken
Leaves us both feeling broken
Let's fight the fight with all our might
To Win would be just the token !

We're all feeling a bit flat
Re-group let's wait and see
You're going nowhere darling
Cos you mean the World to me !

3/07/2013

We will C...

C is for Cancer
C is for cure
Curl up and die
Cos C is insecure
Cometh the hour
Cometh the day
Cometh the time when the C's gone away
C not so big
C you're a pain
C can die off be flushed down the drain
C won't be long be a thing of the past
C we are closing the net we have cast
C is for cured
C is for class
C you've been caught and dumped on your arse.
C is for cadge
C is for crime
C you've been sentenced
C now do your time

03/11/13

Driving

(to visit my Sue in hospital when we were told that she had been cured)

I'm driving feel I'm skiving
When my heart skips a beat I'm thriving
To the place in my mind that plays a huge part
From my soul to my feet I'm jiving

This journey's a learning curve
Certain obstacles we will swerve
My engine's cool like a heated pool
All I care about is my love

My pulse is like a piston
Timing's right and I ain't missed one
She's cured and free of pain
Pure oil running through her veins

I now can't wait to get there
My vision's great not impaired
I've found the core, feelings so sure
In love we make a great pair

10/06/11

What a Day

We went to the Marsden today
For a couple of hours no long stay
Her bloods were spot on
She could do no wrong
I let out an inner Hooray

The trial drug has settled down
It behaved like a rogue on the town
The side effects stalling
She's no longer crawling
Releasing the crease in her frown

The Doctor says you may go
Until next week go with the flow
Today you look fine
In fact really sublime
You are really starting to glow

We take it a week at a time
Tonight it's a lager and lime
For Sue it's green tea
Some fruit cake on her knee
And pray next week she's going to be fine.

It's only the start of the week
I just want to lay down and sleep
And wish her good health
As your health is your wealth
When she conquers it, oh what a treat !

25/11/13

Richard the Lionheart

Richard Corrall - Faith Healer & Friend

We met you a while ago with your lovely dad in tow
With dog Max in the back not on the roof rack
The seeds we began to sow.

You kindly came to treat my Sue
Exploring pastures new
Your hands on approach like a gleaming broach
Left her feeling brand new.

It's really quite amazing
You work as if you're grazing
In your comfort zone - like a dulcet tone
Like a path to health engraving.

Sometimes in your life you meet people for a reason
The energy and care you show
Throughout the whole four seasons

Can only be a good thing with your positive mind
To anyone lucky enough to cross your path
You are a real find.

So thank you for your kindness right from start
A friend indeed with not an ounce of greed
With a real kind Lionheart.

03/11/2013

'C' BOMB

That 'F' in awful letter 'C'
Will always cause a tremor
Yet A to Z are not a threat
Like a Fiver or a Tenner

Nothing much has changed
As your Doctor's Oh so hopeful
You're the one to now stand firm
As all the positives will total !

You're such a ball of fun
A great wife and loving mum
Now is the time for you to shine
And kick 'C' up the bum !

From what I've learned from Col
You're a real seasoned trooper
Who will fight the fight come day and night
Cos you are truly super

Teamwork is the essence
Never feel on your own
Cos many times in others
Some are all alone

A problem shared is a problem halved
Well as the saying goes
As a team you are united
With your spirit how it shows.

As I said at the beginning
'C' is just a letter
You will fight it toe to toe
Just like a soldier go one better

When the fight is over
And you have trounced the sinner
That Cancer 'C' was all a front
Now young lady, you're the Winner !

Moment of Sadness

I'm thinking on the hour, a piece of me's devoured
My heart's ripped out I have self doubt
I'm like a leaning tower

How can you be so intrusive, so callous and abusive
Take my girl today, blue clouds gone grey
Then make it so conclusive

I'm feeling all alone for the first time in my life
Some thoughts I have are very bad
What is the point in life

To keep my tears in tow, like standing in a row
Like a production line tuned oh so fine
Giving a constant flow

Each day I ask the question to fathom it I try
No answers soon on earth or moon
My pillow's wet not dry.

There is no worse a feeling sat here all alone
No Sue to love offer my glove
Cos now my dove has flown.

Don't worry now my darling you're done and free of pain
It's down to me and Tiffany
Love and respect we'll gain !

21/03/14

Wally

There he was sat all alone
Talking to the floor
When I got close I stood and listened
It was to his wife he so adored

He sat there trimming roses
And weeding whilst in thought
His heart was clearly broken
Whilst sat there he did talk

In his light green coat
And faded old blue jeans
A hearing aid around one ear
An old man not a teen

As I walked past him with Tiff
She dug her heels in
He looked up with a broad smile
Then laughed 'She ain't going'

We stood and had a chat
Wally is his name
A fifty four and a half year marriage
That's now ended what a shame

He explained she had a fall
She tripped and then she fell
In hospital they dropped the bomb
She was living cancer hell

Sadly for Wally
He's left to fend and fight
I feel for me yet feel for him
It's a sad old World. Good night

21/03/14

Well Done Dad

(When my Dad returned home from surgery following cancer diagnosis in 2017)

You are really quite unique
Old school and divine
The way you've handled this whole event
You truly are sublime !
When I'm feeling low
Thinking what you've just been through
I revert to your 'genius line' '
We're from good stock - we will pull through'

That sits at the back
Of my overactive brain
But enthuses me in times of doubt
And eases mental pain !
You are our natural leader
And lead by sheer example
With what was dealt some would melt
But you questioned the sample !

Just look at you now
Positive now back home
Archie back on your lap for an occasional pat
Waiting for a bone
You're getting back to normal
Which really is superb
John and Archie, happy family
"I'm watching EastEnders" – *"do not disturb"* !

25/11/13

Thames Hospice

The passing of my Father
27th March, 2017

I'm sat here with my father
To see his passing through
Your team of darling Angels
Are standout from the queue

Each and every one of you
Clearly do it from your hearts
To relax the ones in lesser health
Until they then depart !

It takes a very special person
To do the work you do
Some through the day then through the night
Some start with the morning dew !

You are the unsung heroes
As you always give your all
All your patients under your roof
Are made to feel so tall !

Thank you so much for your kindness
For keeping his dignity intact
For all your care and miles of smiles
Thank you from me and my Dad - that's a fact !

SADNESS

'Small' Spring is in the Air

I woke up this morning
With a small spring in my step
Then things started dawning
Don't say no say yep !

For you Mickey Brown
Have had a Jewel and Treasure
And been in love with the wonderful Sue
Had fifteen years of pleasure

When I look back over the years
With laughter love and pride
I'm so honoured with my choice
Our love we could not hide

I felt ecstatic when I met her
For she was so stand-out
So pure and sure yet so demure
With such an element of clout

Not only stunning on the outside
Like a diamond on a princess
But as stunning on the inside
Became her trait and no less

No wonder it's so hard
To digest my Susan's fate
But I'm the proudest man upon this earth
To say she was my date

27/03/14

My Mate Scrubble

(On losing his wife) 2021

My mind's been racing overtime
Now I'm at the start
Support, Respect I can now reflect
Delivered from the heart

You have been through the wringer
In more ways than one
You've polished your shield, took to the field
Nine out of ten you've won

The one out of ten you've lost
Through no fault of your own
Out of your control it bit your soul
Now your dove has flown

You are a born leader
Once the new kid on the block
You're now older, wise with loyal eyes
Just proves you're from great stock

You have what seems like a mountain
In these coming days
You will take each step to the summit
And walk away with praise

Look what you've achieved together
A smile to lift the mood
In Tobi, George, Jessie now baby Harris too
Your legacies, your brood

Life was never meant to be easy
As we've witnessed on the way
But you my friend will again mend
Starting from today

We're all rooting for you Scrubble
Stay strong cos we're all here
So polish that shield and take to the field
With no element of fear

Breakfast at Tiffany's

How am I feeling today
Ok in my very own way
The scotch hit the spot
And stopped the old rot Hic !
Now are we in April or May

Funny old time on my Jack
Spending evenings flat on my back
It numbs the old pain
Or is it in vain
Again shortly I'll be hitting the sack

Well my Tiff she now shares my bed
Where we snuggle and lay down our heads
It's nice and secure
Cos she's so demure
Midnight feasts include pasties from Greggs

It's my Tiffany's Birthday hooray
I'm so pleased in a funny old way
A Celebration's in order
We will be touching the border
As her Pet passport is well on its way

The saying one man and his dog
You can throw her a stick in the fog
She's more loyal than most
Sniffing my marmite on toast
All of a sudden it's my lap she will hog

Oh well my day's better than some
No real hangover from Whisky or Rum
We will cut Tiffany's cake
Made from kidney and steak
Fed and watered we'll now bang the drum !

25/05/14

Pixie

We've known you since a kitten
Your parents both smitten
On meeting you amongst a few
Our love for you was bitten

A stunning cat you were
With that cool infectious Purr
The colours stand out and full of clout
With your soft and gentle fur !

You always had a new bird
In your mouth brought in the house
As a present for your Mum and Dad
A rat and the occasional mouse !

You are 'King of the Road'
That will always be your title
With your miaow just somehow
Was always such a pure recital !

Today we are all so sad
As the end for you is here
What a brilliant cat sat on our mat
With no element of fear

Pixie today you start your new life
Free from all those aches and pains
It's the ones in us you leave behind
That cry sadness through our veins !

You both have been amazing
To Pixie your loving friend
Even my little girl Tiffany
Loved him in the end

So here's to one stunning cat
We send our love to you
Rest peacefully legend Pixie
Now go say Hi to Sue !

P.C.

After the sad Loss of His Parents
2016

Where do I begin
I guess right from the start
You know me, my mate P.C.
I write straight from the heart

What you are going through is oh so very rough
It grinds you down, draws tears and frowns
It's now you need your inner tough.

There's no rules and regulations
To how you deal with this
If you need an ear you know I'm here
The opportunity please don't miss.

All I want to say is don't run before you can walk
Just take your time the sun will shine
We're all here if you want to talk !

CELEBRITIES

Mega Dump

'I'm A Celebrity 2013'

Big Mo was lodged on the Dunny
To her camp mates it was rather funny
The dump was a log the size of my dog
In pounds it would come to some money

(25/11/13)

Pardon? Eh, what did you say?

(Alan Carr MBE off to a meeting regarding the John Lennon Gypsy Caravan…He left his hearing aid on his desk…)

He's Alan Carr my mucker
Like Polo and a Chucka
A team we are like a classic car
We purr cos we're both pucka

When he's roaming in the garden
To Margaret's screams it's 'Pardon'
Come in for tea … 'What half past three?'
With his selective hearing Jargon

He should have this attachment
Firmly clipped around his ear
But it's no use left on his desk
It did bring my worst fear

Imagine sat in talks
With the king from Dubai
Negotiating Charitable terms
Lennon's Caravan we Cry

"Pardon, what did you say?
Can you speak up cos I'm mutton
To this deal if I hear right
I'm about to press the button"

'No' Alan you misheard
Don't take in all that flannel
You've just agreed to deal
On two Goats, a Yak and Camel

The Lennon Caravan
Well it's part of Rock n roll
Now keep your plastic hearing aid
So close about your soul

You were given eyes to see
And legs so you can walk
If you can't hear what's going on
You won't know when to talk

Now to cut to the chase
I'm giving it a rest
Keep it wrapped around your lobe
Not left upon your desk !

09/06/21

Team Ditcheat

*After Bryony Frost won the Ryanair Chase on Frodon at
Cheltenham, March 2017*

Great words to describe her
For one she's total class
The nicest girl from the inside out
With such talent on the grass !

To see her win at Cheltenham
And win it with such grace
And complement her Frodon
With a huge smile upon her face !

Pegasus he is !
Without a shadow of a doubt
Whilst 'B' sat in the plate like glue
Adding extra clout !

The crowd they roared and cheered
To the ride of the week
To see 'B' in her element
Salute her mount with rosy cheeks !

Team Ditcheat you're amazing
Paul Nicholls you're a Star
Clifford, Kate and Rose to name just a few
Now queue up at the bar !

In the cold and frosty mornings
The wind and rain and snow
Your loyal team there, day in day out
To put on this perfect show !

A Ryanair for Bryony
With Frodon enjoy your fame
Team Ditcheat you're all amazing
Clearly Top of the Game !

The Gypsy King

Tyson Fury, World Heavyweight Champion
Feb 2020

Round One you're incredible man !
On a mission for your army of fans
You don't do treason you're here for a reason
Adored by Paris and your kids Bang Bang !

Once in a lifetime
Legends rise and raise their head
There's Mohammad Ali who was pulling up trees
World titles soon put to bed !

Your Father John's amazing
To the point and there's no phasing
His heart's so true instilled in you
You're his life in your fights he's praising !

You're The Gypsy King no bling
Just proved you're the King of the ring
You're the people's choice - well what a voice
How well can our World Champ sing !

To have been where you've been
Drinking through the Devil's spleen
To come back from the rot with a precision plot
You and yours now deserve the dream !

Tyson you've shown such dedication
Just proved one thing to your Nation
That your mental health has become your wealth
You're an inspiration with accreditation !

When it comes to family ties
Dad John screams pure pride through his eyes
He's the best you'll meet as a dad discreet
May be older but like a barn owl wise

In the fight game your Dad's so proud
You're proven from good stock
With your Paris too - she fits that shoe
That's why team Fury Rocks !

Caroline Flack

My tribute to Caroline

It's nothing short of tragic
With Caroline dead at 40
Her mental health just like a stealth
Swept in, took her life so shortly !

Clearly on the outside
She was open full of laughter, fun
On the inside screaming help me !
For what I'm told I've done !

Our country mourns another young life
So sad so bad so tragic
When disturbed trolls act like pin dolls
To get their sick fix like Black Magic !

She now has no defence
In her mind her problems are over
The trolls think they've won but we're not done
Caroline had both a three and four leaf clover !

What more can one say
Her family and friends have lost a star
Please rest in peace, now they've had their feast
You won, so au revoir !

Voice is the Choice

(Top National Hunt Horse Racing Trainer Nicky Henderson
who trained 'Forgotten Voice')
Congratulations on your brilliance with 'Forgotten Voice'
You are quite clearly the man at the top of your game.

In the morning I flick through the post
While digesting my marmite on toast
I follow your team, then live the dream
On Sunday its red wine with our roast.

What a training feat to the letter
Jonny Murtagh a real go-getter
With Forgotten Voice his number one choice
You couldn't ask for much better !

You're a man at the top of your game
A rarity to be out of the frame
Whether jumpers or flat I must tip my hat
You deserve every ounce of your fame

29/06/13

MENTAL HEALTH

LOSING IT

2010

I wake up in the morning tumble out of bed
Not knowing who I am with, shooting pains in my head
I need my teeth to get hold of the bit
Cos at this time in my life I'm certainly LOSING IT !

I tumble down the stairs to have a slice of toast
Flick the switch the kettle's on, I feel better off than most
My heart starts thumping I feel a lost soul
My head has started spinning I'm OUT OF CONTROL

I go to walk out of the door, full of good intentions
Try to get my life on track, head full of new inventions
My mouth goes dry I'm feeling weak and dead
My heart synchronizes with the BEATS IN MY HEAD

I crawl back up the stairs to where I know the score
My heart rate lowers, I no longer feel the chore
I ain't earnt a dollar, the thought I've gone and tossed it
But one thing's for sure I HAVE DEFINITELY LOST IT !!!

Always Got A Chance

When you're sitting on your own
In a room that's dumb and quiet
Your head is racing fast
And about to start a riot!
Sometimes it's so hard
To feel on a natural high
The realities of life set in
Dig deep, go on please try

Never feel that you're alone
On what seems a long and lonely walk
Pick up the phone and share your tone
Friends are only glad to help and talk
So many people get these feelings
Just exactly as you may
Me for one I didn't know where to run
I'm now feeling stronger by the day

Please don't feel you're any different
To the person stood or sat beside you
Just relax, breathe deep even have a good weep
You will come back stronger too.

Life is so precious I want to share this story
It's an achievable goal that will unfold
And help you in your personal quest for glory

When your life is going nowhere
Or you're just a little lost
Try to keep on smiling
At whatever it may cost
And if you're downing in appearance
Please stand up and make a stance
Because when you smile the world smiles with you
And you've *Always Got A Chance*

One Life, Live it

A confidence boost to young art student Sam after I saw his
stunning piece of artwork

Confidence is key here when I'm screaming of self-doubt
Those around me make the perfect sounds, it's me that's in a drought
Art runs through my veins, it's in my blood and D.N.A.
So why the hell do I doubt myself in life from day to day

I look at others work and respect the top of the tree
I just need that break and given chance, 'Hey world what about me' !

I understand the process, but this process takes its time
I am so ready now, let me go I'll pay the fine
Lately I'm treading treacle, always waiting on instruction
When in my heart I'm pumping iron, I don't do self-destruction

There is no age limit, to be a Super Star
I'm ready in the starting blocks, I will win this race by far !

There's been times of frustration, I'm now prepared to take that chance
To show my work to mainstream Toffs and take that moral stance

I know I have the skill set, maybe that is why I'm loved
So all you pushy doubting mugs, lets now take off the gloves !

If it works in what I'm doing great, if not at least I had a go
Whether Arts and Crafts or any other trade, leave me to find my flow
I've arrived on the scene from an acorn to an oak tree
Ladies and Gents there is a queue, now please kindly stand behind me !

HUMOUR

Weight Watchers

Really?
'I'll eat to that !'

I signed in at Weight Watchers
To do something about my weight
The pen I used was tasty
Like a coffee walnut cake
I sat in the chair
Whilst she stared with such a frown
As I flicked the top of my Kentucky Box
My mentor grilled me up and down

As I ripped into my purchase, four thighs and a wing
The fries were also so de-lish, it made my pallet sing !
"There's no hope for you Sir ! You're on a slippery slope'"
As I washed it down with a banana shake she clearly couldn't cope

She reminded me of a twiglet as she sat sucking on a grape
There was more meat on a toothpick, I found her rather fake
As I finished my last mouthful and slouched back in the chair
She refused to stand me on the scales; my experience ended there !

She bragged "I've lost ten stone, and now I'm only three"
I said I do that in a morning dump after a cup of tea!
She was losing patience so I slipped on my coat
I found some toffees in my pocket, they soon went down my throat.

Well the thought was there, so I have to say
Weight Watchers clearly not for me, certainly not today
So she saw me to the door, the wind nearly blew her over
I thought it's fish and chips for me tonight with a sole from Dover!

Superhali Fragilistic Smells Like Halitosis

Superhali Fragilistic Smells Like Halitosis
You can tell by the smell of it
It's really quite atrocious
If you say it pongs enough
You'll knock people unconscious

Superhali Fragilistic Smells Like Halitosis

HUM-dittle-ittl-Hum-dittle-I
HUM-dittle-ittl-Hum-dittle-I
HUM-dittle-ittl-Hum-dittle-I
HUM-dittle-ittl-Hum-dittle-I

Now he is afraid to speak
Cos it is so sad
Like a Michael Jackson song
They sniff and say who's Bad !
But then the chemist opens
The staff are on their toes
He fills his bags with Listermint
When he speaks they hold their nose

Superhali Fragilistic Smells Like Halitosis
You can tell by the smell of it
It's really quite atrocious
If you say it pongs enough
You'll knock people unconcious

Superhali Fragilistic Stinking Halitosis !

To fade *(faint)* …
A honking production !

Justice

2012

I wake up in the morning get into my car
Drive down to my local cafe for a nice strong cuppa cha
Study the Racing Post to pick out my daily banker
There's a bastard clamping firm, what a load of merchant flankers

I supp my tea and leave the cafe, one eye on the firm
Did I park in a disabled bay? My tummy starts to churn
It's been my slot for five years and I never got no agg
I'm clearly out of luck today, on my screen's a plastic bag

I peel off the sticker, nearly taking out my screen
It will never be the same with a spray of Mister Sheen
I follow the instructions - I ain't going nowhere
I slip back in for a bacon roll and get comfy in my chair

Planning my revenge I ring the local plant hire firm
"The best oxyacetylene gun you've got, can you deliver for a turn?"
"Oh yes, one set of goggles" as I cannot risk arc eye
I will cut the clamp and weld it to his dish installed by Sky

Would it have been easier just to pay the fine?
Like sex on the beach with your first love, the pleasure's been all mine
These grubby thieving bastards who would even sell their gran
They can all now go to hell in their shitty rusty van.

Hair Hair

My Father (HJC) had strong views about beards

What is their reason
For that mass of facial hair
To impersonate a coconut
Or a raging Grizzly Bear

Now is it necessary
To cover both head and chin
The only one that benefits
Is the one that's paid to trim

I have to ask myself
And be it rather crude
Is it like a mobile pantry
Where one stores his excess food

A beard is so weird
Just a fuzzy clump of hair
Where is the trend in that
Surely a lack of care !

All our global sporting icons
Especially in track and field
Would clearly beat their personal bests
Without this dreadful shield
If you have to grow a beard
Then just make it a Brazilian
Just a little strip on your chin tip
To complement our Gillian !

As H.J.C. has always stated
Why hide behind a beard
Then they go and buy a Volvo estate
He always found it rather weird

With all the uncertainty
When it comes to the ladies - don't faze her
Get yourself down to your local store
And buy a bleedin' razor !

29/05/2017

Team Rosebank

Tiffany's trip to the Vets

Good Morning Rosebank Cottage
And thank you all so much
Gill you made me better to the letter
You have the perfect touch !

I am a tiny fawn Chihuahua
And WOW was I in pain
With dodgy teeth I couldn't chew my food
They went against the grain

Like most naughty doggies
I rarely clean my teeth
Just the odd bone whilst sat at home
From our local butcher Keith

I woke up this morning
Had my normal shake in style
Glanced as I passed in the full length glass
Gill you've given me back my perfect smile !

Thank you for your kindness
I'm off out on the town
Team Rosebank you're amazing
All my love from Tiffany Brown !

02/03/19

To My Editor, The Lovely Coleen

2021

I will give you a clue, comma
Who I'm referring to full stop.
She checks it with a tooth comb
Exclamation mark on top !

Open "inverted commas"
To start her next statement
Closed "inverted commas"
With storms continuing without abatement

New paragraph now Mickey
Start with a Capital Letter
Then a hyphen here - and a hyphen there -
Your punctuation's so much better

I know you're only trying to help me
I appreciate your advice
Now can we get the pâté from the fridge
And spread it on a slice !